Stephen Cottrell is the Bisho, ...g. ..s many books include *I Thirst* (Zondervan 2003), the Archbishop of Canterbury's Lent Book for 2004, *From the Abundance of the Heart: Catholic evangelism for all Christians* (DLT 2006); *Do Nothing to Change your Life: Discovering what happens when you stop* (CHP 2007) and, most recently, *The Adventures of Naughty Nora* (BRF 2008), a collection of stories for children. He is married to Rebecca and they have three boys.

The Things He Carried

A journey to the cross:
meditations for Lent and Holy Week

STEPHEN COTTRELL

First published in Great Britain in 2008

Society for Promoting Christian Knowledge
36 Causton Street
London SW1P 4ST

British Library Cataloguing-in-Publication Data
A catalogue record for this book is available from the British Library

ISBN 978–0–281–06080–1

5 7 9 10 8 6 4

Designed and typeset by Kenneth Burnley, Wirral, Cheshire
First printed in the UK by CPI Bookmarque, Croydon, CR0 4TD
Reprinted in the UK by Ashford Colour Press

Produced on paper from sustainable forests

For all those carrying heavy burdens

Surely he has borne our infirmities
(Isaiah 53.4)

Contents

Introduction

The inspiration for this book came first from Tim O'Brien's collection of short stories reflecting on his time in Vietnam called *The Things They Carried*. In these stories we don't just hear about the physical things that the soldiers carry, but also their terrors and dreams. Even as I was reading this book I was starting to wonder about the things that Jesus carried: not just the cross itself, but the crown of thorns he was forced to wear, the seamless robe that was taken from him, the other burdens that we laid upon him, and also the hopes and fears that he carried in his heart and that are reflected in the different passion narratives we read in scripture. Then in 2005 I was asked to preach for the Good Friday 'Three Hours' service at St Paul's Cathedral. A big preach indeed! I wondered whether an examination of the things that Jesus carried might be a good way of re-presenting the story of the passion and help get inside both the feelings and the meaning. Those Good Friday reflections have now been expanded and developed into this book.

As I have written I have imagined myself at the cross. I have striven for a way of writing that is more meditative than analytical; more poetry than prose. (I even wonder whether you might consider reading it aloud to yourself!) Obviously the scriptures are my primary inspiration; but in taking liberties with the letter of the text (and daring to suggest I can tell you how Jesus might have felt) I have tried to write something that will get inside the spirit of the story and offer a vessel for your own feelings and questions. Hence, at the end of each chapter there are some suggestions for reflection. This can either be done on your own, or in a group with others. In this process, I hope the book will stimulate thought, provoke discussion and create space for contemplation. In order to understand the cross you need to stand under it. This has to be done with the imagination as well as the mind. With heart as well as head. This book aims to help in this process of standing under. But however you use it – on your own or with others – I hope you will receive some small appreciation of just how much the cross weighs, and maybe even pick it up yourself.

1

The cross

He carried a large wooden beam – one half of a cross.

They handed it to him like it was nothing. Like it could be thrown away; like they were going to throw *him* away, this thing of terrible beauty.

He held the rough wood in his hands; gripped it, felt its shape, tested its weight, imagined the plane upon it, the axe striking the base of the trunk, the weight of the leaves upon the branches fluttering in the air of a spring day, breathing their last, gasping, falling, crashing down. He saw it dragged away, cut open, dissected, used.

He remembered its growing in the forest. A tiny unfolding. The first leaf unravelling. Felt the sap rising within it: its growing, and its vast potential. He felt its density. This was the hull of a boat, the rafters of a house, the handle of a plough, the shaft of an axe. It contained the strength to support and the durability to hold. It contracted and expanded. It was eye of a needle. It was base of a table. And now a grim vocation: to be the place where death is distributed.

3

And no one would look him in the eye: not at this point; not as this broad beam was handed out. This was the time to look away, to scan the horizon and search for a new sail. This was the time to think of home and hearth, of logs being thrown on the fire.

He shouldered the weight. It could carry him and it could crush him. He felt its roughness against his rawness. The splinters that pushed into his flesh anticipated the nails that were to follow. It was fruit of the earth and the work of human hands, this wood he carried.

It was half a cross. He didn't carry the whole thing, though that was how it would usually be remembered. But nobody ever got him right. And he always evaded those who clung too tightly. Just the crosspiece which his hands would be nailed to: he carried it. And he knew that when he reached the place of execution a stake would be ready, and the beam attached to it; and his hands nailed to it – actually his wrists, in-between the bones, so that the flesh wouldn't tear, and he could hang there longer. He would be hoisted up. It would make a cross; and then his feet would be nailed in place.

But first there was a journey to make: from Pilate's palace, through the crowded city streets, to the hill of the skull outside the walls, about half a mile. And all this way he half-carried, half-dragged this great girder, this joist from which he would hang.

4

It was about five feet in length – the height of a small person. It weighed about five stone – as much as a bag of cement. And he was already battered and broken from being flogged. And the crowd that had welcomed him days earlier now bayed for blood. And the pallor and expectancy of death was already upon him.

He emptied himself, taking the form of a slave . . .

He humbled himself and became obedient to the point of death . . .

The Romans were fond of crucifixion. It was their execution of choice. They liked its precision. It produced the maximum amount of pain and a death struggle of adjustable duration. They had so mastered this technology of killing that they could decide how much it hurt and how long it lasted. The clever bit was the nail through the feet. A body just suspended by the wrists will soon develop agonizing cramp. The ribs are drawn upwards and the chest is fixed in position as if the victim has just drawn a large breath, but cannot breathe out. The metabolic rate surges and within an hour or so the victim dies of suffocation. But by nailing the feet the condemned man could buy time by pushing himself up on the nails and by stretching his legs could raise his body a few inches and relieve the tension in his chest and arms.

But perching with the full weight of your body on a square nail driven though the middle bones of your feet brings intolerable pain. The victim soon lets his knees sag and is once more hanging from the wrists, and so the cycle repeats itself, over and over again, sometimes for as long as three days. Death comes slowly.

And everyone knew about crucifixion. Over a thousand years thousands of people died this way. There were times when the Romans' circus arenas became forests of crosses.

As he carried this weight through the streets Jesus knew what was in store for him.

We imagine him, stumbling through the narrow, crowded alleys of Jerusalem on a hot, humid Friday afternoon: we sense the frenzied animation of the crowd; we see the spite-ful excitement etched into the faces of those who shout and jeer; we feel their spittle on our face; we see their hands waving, their fingers jabbing; we smell the rank odour of blood and sweat; we feel the weight of the cross pressing us down; and then we hear the blood lust of the crowd boil over. We know in our hearts how easy it is to run with the crowd, and we know how we would have responded. With horror, we see it is our hands upon him; our fingers point-ing; our voices jeering.

And then we see him fall – as if in slow motion – tumbling, stumbling, reaching out for a support that has been taken away, vanquished: his hands sliding in the dust, straining for purchase; the beam itself crashing down, the crowd laughing, the soldiers who accompany him pointing, heaving him to his feet, bidding him continue.

And suddenly it seems to mean nothing. Another useless dreamer. He is just another innocent man going to his death, like so many thousands and millions of other innocent people have died ugly and anonymous deaths through the whole bloody failure of human history – in gas chambers, killing fields, firing squads, trenches, collapsing buildings, atomic explosions, bombed trains, the list goes on and on. Two million men, women and children in Hiroshima, six million in Nazi death camps . . . How many by Stalin, or Pol Pot, or in Rwanda, or Kosovo, or Darfur, or all those barbarous killings that we cannot remember where whole communities were wiped out? And here he is, one more man going to his death, silent before his accusers, stoical in his suffering, useless to stem the flow of hatred and revenge that consumes the human heart. After the defeat of the Spartacus uprising in 71 BC, 6,500 rebellious slaves were crucified. Their crosses lined the Appian Way from Cappadocia to Rome. Their names are forgotten, as in the end all names are forgotten. But the carpenter's son from Nazareth – this man stumbling to this death – he is remembered. And of all the things we remember about his life and teaching, it is this event – his dying – that we remember most. It is why you are reading this book. And the means of his death – the cross – we remember it. Why? Is it because this man is not just a man – not less than a man, but God contained within what it is to be man? And is his suffering and his dying not just one more notch carved in the endless torment of human misery, but God sharing it, God involved in the world he made, God stretched out on this fearful piece of wood?

When I am lifted up . . .

He is face to face now with our barbarity. He carries the cross, and he treads a path of suffering, step by painful step, that is the suffering of the world. He carries the battered woundedness of everyone who has been trapped and convicted by the foul depravity of all the awfulness we do to each other. He can taste its breath. He can feel its hands upon him. But he carries something else. A light flickering within him that will not be snuffed out. Not when the soldiers mock him; not when he is stripped and beaten; not when they drive in the nails; not when he hangs there ridiculed, forsaken, defeated. He carries half a cross; that half which is God's determination to plumb the depths of that dark river which is the human heart. But the other half is entirely something else: something that also needs to be nailed down and joined up. He is reaching into the bloody mess in order to redeem it. He carries the purposes of God. They will be shaped into a cross.

For reflection

Hold a piece of wood. Imagine where it came from. Imagine it growing in the forest. Imagine who cut it down and who shaped it into this thing you are holding.

If you are in a group, ask each person to bring something made of wood. Show each other what you have brought. Talk about how it was made and where it came from.

If you are on your own, just hold the wood and think about it.

Hold something heavy. Feel its weight. Hold it for as long as possible, until you can hardly hold it any longer.

If you are in a group, pass the weighty object from one person to the next. Afterwards talk about how it felt.

If you are on your own, just hold it and think about its weight.

Read Mark 15.6–15. Then ask these questions:

1   How does it feel to be overburdened?

2   What is the heaviest load?

3   What is the greatest pain?

4   What does it mean to say the cross is a thing of beauty?

2

A crown of thorns

H
e carried a crown of thorns.

The soldiers' logic had a brutal simplicity. A cruel, school-boy logic. He said he was a king, so dress him up as one. A purple robe. Some twisted thorn. A makeshift crown. Briers and acacia. The barbed wire of the bush. Harvest it gingerly. Put that in your pipe and smoke it. Stack him up. Salute him. Stretch him. Strike him. Scratch him. Scar him. Skewer him. Scoff and mock him. And afterwards the grazed hands of the harvesters plunged into basins of cool water for relief. And smiling at each other, wink and reminisce. A cracking good joke.

They made him a kind of pantomime king. Something to laugh at. Something to scorn. They bowed before him and grinning they worshipped him. Then they beat him.

They had their way with him. They made fun of him in the way that bullies easily do when there is someone defenceless in their midst. Someone who won't fight back. Someone who's a bit different. Someone who makes claims that are easy to mock. His silence convicts him. That's how they see it. A loser. (And lest we start imagining how we would have

13

been so different, let's be honest about the bully inside us. How easy it is to make fun of others. To laugh at someone else's downfall. The joy of immunity. The solidarity of the pack. The savage delights of the kill. Remember the butchery of the playground? The cutting word that split so deep. The carefully rehearsed put-down. The thoughtless slur.)

They wanted him sorted. They wanted him put in his place. But they didn't know where his place was. 'Not of this world' they had heard him say. Well this was one dreamer they would haul back down to earth. They would reel him in. Like Icarus they would watch him flounder and burn. What had his dreams achieved? Just more trouble for them. The crowds were always bad at this time of year, stirred into a ferment of religious excitement and anticipation. He had made matters worse. Did he expect them just to leave? The mighty Roman Empire to roll over? What sort of revolution could this dreamer roll? They could crush him so easily! He was a grasshopper under their feet. They would stamp him out.

And where were his followers? Abandoned him, every one of them. A king, indeed! They would show him. They would do him honour. They would make him a crown.

And dressing Jesus as a king was such a wonderfully good joke that, like all good jokes, like every piece of well-honed gossip, it soon had legs. It travelled down the corridors of

Roman power from soldier to soldier, from slave to slave, from senator to senator. It wormed its way into people's ears, because we are all delighted by intrigue and scandal and love to laugh at some else's ruin. Even to the ears of Pilate. 'Are you a king?' he enquires with a smile. And when he leads him out before the people: 'Here is your King!'

The crowds spit back their curt reply. Laughing. Sneering. We have no King but Caesar.

Pilate then issues instructions for a sign to be put above the cross saying 'Jesus of Nazareth, the King of the Jews'. And so that everyone can get the joke, he decrees that it must be written in three languages – Hebrew, Greek and Latin. All the world can now enjoy the joke. This wretched little preacher from Nazareth said he was a king.

But then the joke reaches the ears of the High Priest. And he isn't laughing. Jesus' silence never quite speaks to him of a broken man; rather he is disturbed by his silence, confronted by his presence: it is almost as if he is judging them. 'Don't put King of the Jews', he intervenes, 'but this man *said* he was King of the Jews.' So they stare each other out. These two big men. These occupying forces: one of the present and one of the past, but neither has the future in control, though they will battle on, oblivious and defiant to the truth the joke reveals. It is too late. The cat is out the bag. It has been uttered. 'What I have written, I have written,' retorts Pilate.

And so Jesus is unwound. Adorned with thorn he wears the crown. And that which was meant to mock reveals the deepest truth.

When I am lifted up from the earth . . .

The joke backfires. He is a king: a piercing beam of light for all the world: the very one that all Israel has been hoping for, waiting for; the one to whom all their scriptures and their prophets point. All the troubled searching of this nomadic nation, their deepest longings and the keenest insights of their brightest minds, has come down to this man, and been refined into this moment. But they don't see it. They laugh out loud instead. And we would have done the same. Even those who have caught a glimpse of who he is are now cowering in fear, hanging onto their own lives and reputations, getting ready to go back to how it was before him.

There is a further twist: those he has come to save now hurry to get a better view of his dying, sneering at his stupidity. What sort of a king is this?

Even as he hangs there, the life draining out of him, the taunts come thick and fast. 'He saved others, but he cannot save himself!' Even one of the criminals crucified with him joins in the fun: 'Save yourself, and us as well,' he scoffs. And in his heart, though no longer on his lips, he carries the words that will get him through the next few hours. 'My kingdom is not from this world. If my kingdom were from this world, my followers would be fighting to keep me from being handed over. But as it is, my kingdom is not from here.'

'So you are a king?' The words of Pilate beat against him.

'For this I was born and for this I came into the world, to testify to the truth. Everyone who belongs to the truth listens to my voice.' And behind this the agony of vocation: 'Father, if it is possible, take this cup away from me.'

But there is no other way. All the supports have been removed. This is a cup that must be drained to the dregs. He stands at a point of terrible isolation, a crux. Behind him the baying of the mob. Ahead of him only wood and twisted thorn. Derision and decision. The wood he carries is the sign of his inclusive participation in the suffering of the world. He will now take his place at this bloody banquet. The thorn is a sign that he is what he is: anointed and annihilated, what so few people saw him to be – only children and demons – the Messiah of God; and that God's redeeming will be accomplished in the bloody horror of his dying. Not that God gains any pleasure from this death. This is not some ghastly bargain being brokered in pain. Both God and man are forsaken in this emptying out of love.

The thorns press harder. Blood pumps from the punctured skin, oozes, clots in the heat and the sweat, and flows again.

He is faint. His hands are shaking. He slips and falls again. Out of reach. Utterly alone.

The Godhead which is fully alive in Jesus, the crucified, is poured into the lap of uncomprehending humanity. These are the truths the thorns reveal. All our deaths and all our sorrows and all our failures are nailed to this tree. This is our half of the cross. We die with him because he chose to die with us. He carries a crown that all can wear; and the cross itself is our escape from the snare, a way to travel.

The darkness beckons. The flies buzz around his face. Still the crowds taunt: 'Let the Messiah, the King of Israel, come down from the cross so that we may see and believe.' But how could he come down? The cross that he carries is his throne. He is reigning from the tree.

For reflection

Hold a piece of holly, or something else which is sharp or prickly. See how carefully it must be held or harvested to prevent it pricking your flesh.

If you are in a group carefully pass the holly from one person to the next.

If you are on your own, just hold it and think about it.

Read Mark 15.16–20. Then ask these questions:

1   How does it feel to be ridiculed?

2   What are the sharpest words?

3   What does it mean to say Jesus is King?

3

A seamless robe

He carried a seamless robe.

It was a thing of delicate beauty and of great craftsmanship, robust and at the same time light, woven in one piece from top to bottom; like the robe a high priest would wear as he went about his duties.

Like everything else, it would be taken from him.

Freshly made, it billowed from the loom as it was released, completed. The freshness and the newness of it made you want to bury yourself in its folds. Or else just put it on. The fingers that spun it, the hands that made it, held together in satisfaction of a job well done. For things crafted have a lasting value: but one that is easily squandered. Mass production leaves little space for the tiny detail that makes this thing this and that thing that. Or it is just plain compromised by cheap labour and the lust to possess everything.

Laundered and hung out to dry it drifted in the breeze like a flag.

But there was no breeze that day. The air seemed to hang in the sky like a great, leaden weight; like the yellowing clouds of smog that stain our own cities. Somewhere a fire was crackling. Dogs barked. Children cried out in fear or stared in bemused amazement.

His sweat and blood stained the cloth. It clung to him, and where he had been lashed, the fibres of the material stuck to the congealing wounds.

Around the hem, where the stitching was plain to see, the material was starting to fray. Something was unravelling, becoming undone.

And on another day, in another crowd, one would reach out to touch this hem. Not to admire its beauty, or measure the quality of the cloth, but to come as close as one could to touching the man; to feel his pulse and know the energy of his life. And even in a crowd, with hundreds jostling around him, clamouring for attention, he would cry out, 'Who touched me?', as if this were something obvious. But he could tell. He could be pressed in on every side and still discern each touch. You see, there are no crowds for him, only people, each one a thing of beauty, each one delicately and unrepeatedly distinct. He sees each face, knows each name, feels each touch and knows its meaning.

What do you want me to do for you . . .

Unless I wash you, you have no share with me . . .

Soon there will be rough hands upon him, uncomprehending and uncaring. No one dies with their clothes on. And if
it wasn't so lovely they would have torn it off him, as though
they were raping him, but it was too costly, too comely.
So suddenly they were gentle. This thing could make them a
few pounds, or keep them warm, or spruce them up, or give
them something to brag about. They rolled it carefully over
his head. They gave this robe a dignity that they did not give
to him, for he was a thing despised and a thing rejected. It
stung as the cloth pulled against the wounds, and then they
held it to themselves smiling, triumphant. And he was left
naked. And now they did not look away. They exposed him.
They smirked at him and they held him to the beam of the
cross ready to secure him.

And when he was nailed there, and when he had been lifted
up, and when the final cycle of the struggle towards dying
had commenced they crouched at the foot of the cross and
spun their dice, gambling to see which one of them would
have it, this seamless robe, this last uncovering.

And he carried the seamless purposes of God: that was what
he was carrying at this moment, though exhaustion and
terror and the raw, uncomplicated torment of dying meant
that he did not need to know he was carrying it, he just had
to do it. He had arrived at a point where there were no

25

choices left, except the one to utter words of gentle forgiveness to those who ducked and dealt, for they too were being
woven into the tapestry of God's story. A seamless purpose:
his birth, his life, the slow unfolding of vocation, the chill
awakening of his baptism, the pleading in the garden for
another way, and now this, his dying, all part of an unfolding hope and a glory that was present in the heart of God
before the world was made. Now planted in *his* heart, turning slowly towards completion, the hour of reckoning, and
as the strange eclipsing darkness gathers, the beckoning of
a new dawn, a new heaven and a new earth. God's work of
redeeming planted in *our* hearts. Those words of forgiveness
spoken to us. Father forgive them, they don't know what
they do.

For reflection

Hold the most beautiful piece of cloth you can find. Imagine who made it and how it was made. Admire and cherish the intricacies of each stitch.

If you are in a group, either get everyone to bring in a piece of cloth, each person showing and sharing what they have brought, or pass around one piece.

If you are on your own, hold the cloth and think about it.

Read John 19.23–25. Then ask these questions:

1   How does it feel to have things of beauty taken away from you?

2   How does it feel to stand alone?

3   What are the worst intrusions?

4   What does it mean to say the cross reveals the purposes of God?

4

His followers' disappointments

He carried his followers' disappointments. You see, they thought he was going to be a different sort of king.

Heaven knows, he had tried. He had tried to etch eternity into the stubborn humanity of those who followed him, but now nearly all of them have abandoned him. Through eyes smarting with grief and narrowed by pain he looks out to see who will listen to the truth that is revealed in his death and there is hardly anyone there: just John, faithful, beloved John. He is still standing. He can also see his mother. She is bent over in grief, her body shaking with tears. Now and then her eyes reach upwards, searching out his gaze. He looks at her. But for once he cannot tell what she is thinking.

Several other women are also there. They seem better equipped to deal with pain than the men. They comfort each other. They hold him in their gaze and he is comforted. His gaze holds them in return. They stand under the cross and they find understanding. Perhaps this is the only way.

His disciples have gone. The shepherd has been struck and the sheep have scattered. Even Peter: pig-headed, big-hearted, bird-brained Peter. He had seen who Jesus was, but he had still got it wrong, railing against his tough words that the Messiah had to suffer and die.

Get behind me Satan . . .

And, no, at that time, he didn't know when, and, yes, he was still struggling to know why, but he also carried the knowledge that he was somehow to be the fulfilment of all God had longed to do through Israel.

Into your hands, Lord, I commit my spirit . . .

That he was a second Adam revealing a new humanity.

That he was a second Moses revealing a new covenant.

And he shuddered with the memory of all the struggle, the torment and the raging against God that had led to this most scandalous and blasphemous conclusion being the truth: that God was in him, and that his purpose was the purpose of God. And how, when you can't fully understand it yourself, are you supposed to tell it to others? Stories and riddles and signs seemed to be the only way. You couldn't persuade people to believe it. You had to wait till the penny dropped. And it was achingly slow.

They were only prepared to go so far. They followed him when he was rebuking the religious leaders for their hypocrisy and cant. They followed him when he fed the multitudes. They followed him when he healed the sick. They followed him when it seemed to them he was a conquering leader. They followed him because they believed he was the Messiah. But they stopped following when they found out what a Messiah really is.

Then they fled. Like a sudden change in the weather, when the promise of a bright day is overtaken by thunder clouds and rain, they were gone. And Peter himself, who had promised that if everyone else deserted he would stand firm, had crumbled, like a house built on sand. He even denied he had ever known him.

And Jesus carried with him the knowledge of that moment: looking into Peter's eyes and seeing the betrayal. And sharing bread with Judas and knowing what he was about to do. And now, almost alone, almost accomplished, wondering: will they ever get it?

He had broken bread with them the night before and given them a way of seeing what the bloody horror of this dying meant; but they are not here to see it; not here to make the connections.

They wanted a different sort of Messiah. He had confounded them, and now they were embarrassed by him, endangered: and so they had left him. They were somewhere in the shadows. Not the shadow of the cross, but the shadow you create yourself when you turn your back on the light. They were nursing their disappointment. Carrying it like a trophy. Complaining how deceived they had been. Soon they would forget. Or else start saying it was better this way. In years to come, when they were fat and fifty, they would lean back in their chairs and smile at the foolishness of youth.

And this was a terrible thing to carry. The thought of it made him wince and retch. He carried the terrible possibility that it was all in vain. That he could walk at their side for ever and never be recognized, never be known; that endless bread would be broken and wine poured out, but incomprehensively, as if it were just food. They would go back to how things were. They would forget. They would airbrush out these crazy years, and, clinging to their portentous hopes of empire and power, look out for the next Messiah to deliver them a kingdom of their own.

And then a more terrible thought – something to be carried that drops like a dead weight in the heart – perhaps he had got it wrong? Perhaps he was not just carrying their vanity, but his own? Perhaps that is all he is carrying – just vanity, foolishness and the unerring certainty of his impending death.

And then the crucified man screams out: 'My God, my God, why have you forsaken me?'

But there is one more indignity to carry. You would laugh if it wasn't so monumentally awful. Even these words are misunderstood. The crowd hear the 'Eli' of his cry to God and think he is saying Elijah. And, like the religious junkies that they are, they suddenly get interested, much preferring a sign from the false gods they persist with than the living God before them. And they say to one another, 'Listen, he is calling for Elijah. Let us see whether Elijah will come and get him down.'

He carries with him the knowledge that even in this moment of utter desolation he is misunderstood. We just don't get it.

For reflection

Hold a sealed envelope. Imagine it contains a letter inform-
ing you of the result of a job interview or an important
examination result. Imagine you are on the brink of elation
or disappointment. Imagine how it feels to not know what
something you are holding holds.

If you are in a group, pass the envelope around.

If you are on your own, just hold it and think about it.

Read Mark 9.30–37. Then ask these questions:

1   How does it feel to be let down?

2   How does it feel to be misunderstood?

3   What is it like to think that all your work might be for
    nothing?

4   What does it mean to say Jesus was human like us?

5

The hopes of God

He carried the hopes of God.

This is how he had come to see it – searching the scriptures, sucking the marrow of wisdom from the very bones of his faith. That God had spent everything to try and create community with his beloved; that is, with us, this sophisticated ape that struts on its hind legs and has dominion over all the world as if he or she were a god, and yet, frail and fallen, a creature not a creator, still bearing God's image. God had spent everything – through covenants, through prophets – everything except himself. And now, when all was exhausted except for the love from which this world was made and which still ached to include within the circle of love that beloved humanity which bore God's mark, there was only one way left: to communicate love in the only language that human beings really understand, the language of a human life. And it was in his life and in his death that this new covenant would be spoken.

This is my servant . . . whom I uphold . . .

This is my son, the beloved, listen to him . . .

These were words from the Father that he carried to sustain him: the belief and the conviction that God was at work in him reconciling the world to himself. And he carried the knowledge that this vocation had not arrived in his lap fully formed, but had been worked out and fought against over many years – nearly thirty. And now it was no longer about what he said – though there were still so many things he longed to say. Nor could it simply be the signs and wonders he performed, though he longed to bring comfort and healing to the confusion and pain that he encountered everywhere and in every human heart. Now it was just about what he did: about carrying this body to this cross on this Friday afternoon and submitting to the malevolence and the odium that would be inflicted upon him.

When he had first begun his ministry, John the baptizer had said of him, 'Look, there is the Lamb of God.' These words had hit him hard and he carried them with him. And now he realized what they meant. He saw it all in painful detail. God was at last making good his promise to Abraham. A lamb for the slaughter was being provided. All he had to do now was be that slaughtered lamb whose shed blood saves. And as his forebears had painted the blood of the Passover lamb on the lintels of their doors to ward off approaching death, so his blood poured out on the lintel of this wood – this door between life and death – would save. And then there would be no more goats or pigeons sliced open; no more entrails burnt; no more the terrifying grip of death upon everything and the endless pleading for mercy from a god made in our own image; pressed into the selfsame straitjacket of anxiety that we are cursed with. (Knowing our nakedness, we could never find enough clothes to wear.) Now there would be no need for any more blood to be spilled. Oh yes, we would spill blood. We like nothing more. But there would never be any need again. Nor would anyone ever be pressed into knowing it. This last sacrifice would really be the end of all of that. (And seeing into the future, carrying all that was to come, he saw for one horrifying moment the elaborate intricacies of how we would butcher the world in the name of this carpenter. How we would dedicate walls in honour of the man who came to break them down.) But now, carrying himself into the inner sanctum, he saw it clearly: it would no longer be necessary for priests to go into the temple year by year to plead to God on humanity's behalf. There would be no more barriers protecting God's presence and keeping us out. No more systems deciding who has favour with God and who does not. This blood will be shed for all. It will be the end of it.

He carries to the cross every person and every person's death. For now every person's death will be the only entrance qualification required. There won't be any other rules. There will be only him: nailed down and lifted up and shining a light through the darkness of death to a banquet where the least and the lost are ushered to the finest seats. And with this he carried all the wild and lovely hopes of God. He carried the

41

possibility of a new temple, and a new covenant and a new relationship. And beyond death, and beyond the rest that is beyond death, he saw a new creation, a new heaven and a new earth. It was as if he were carrying a great table into the banqueting room itself. And planting it in the centre of the room, and pulling out leaf after leaf till it grew and spread. And now placing chairs around the table. Chair after chair, place after place. A vast multitude of places and everyone known. There was no anonymity here. Each was separate – a set place for everyone – and each was connected; round and round the table they would sit, each honoured, each reaching out to serve. Can you conceive it? Every person carried, and every person's death? His heart would break from it. Our minds will reel from it. Our common sense will deny it, but while there is the scrap of possibility that I might find a bit more love in my own feeble heart then surely his heart, fashioned by the heart of God, still beating, can accommodate.

And he carried a new commandment, a new commandment that could be seen in that reciprocity of love that grew around the table – we should love one another with the same love that we see in him. We should expand the dimensions of our hearts. We should let them be filled.

For in him all the fullness of God was pleased to dwell . . .

For he had also planted a table on earth: one that will abide until through the portal of death we take our place at that other table in the new creation. A table where feet are washed and where hearts are fed. A place of receiving; a place to learn from. Yes, Peter had been there. And so had Judas. They had received the bread. Their feet had been washed. Their hearts would be expanded.

Love one another as I have loved you . . .

Love your enemies as yourself . . .

Pray for those who persecute you . . .

If they are thirsty give them something to drink . . .

If someone asks for your coat give your cloak as well . . .

If anyone strikes you on one cheek let them also strike the other . . .

If they force you to walk one mile, walk a second mile as well . . .

This was what he was walking now: the second mile of love. He was oppressed, and he was afflicted, yet he did not open his mouth.

Like a lamb led to the slaughter . . .

Like a sheep that before its shearers is silent, he did not open his mouth . . .

He carried the determination that this new commandment should be lived out, demonstrated, here in his dying, no matter how difficult. This was the moment of disclosure, where the risky enterprise of tenacious love would stand or fall. All God's hopes and all God's purposes were poured into these hours of passion. This was the place where hate would spend itself. There was no fallback position; no Plan B. So, he forgave those whose dismal duty it was to bang home the nails; and he looked with mercy upon those who spat and scoffed and struck out. Not because it was a duty laid upon him, but because he carried in his heart the ways of love. There was no other way.

And again he falls. It is as if he is always falling. Dropping through the air, falling through the earth itself, burrowing down into the very depths of death. How far must he go before everyone is gathered in his arms? To hell itself?

So for the last part of the journey someone else is dragged from the crowd to help shoulder the weight of the cross. And we shudder, fearful that we might be asked to do the same.

For reflection

Hold a bible in your hands. It is the story of the hopes of God and of the response of God's people. Think about what it contains and what it promises. Feel the weight of it.

If you are in a group, pass one bible around.

If you are in your own, just hold it and think about it.

Read Mark 12.1–12. Then ask these questions:

1   What is my part in this story?

2   How does it feel to have a vocation?

3   What sustains us in life?

4   Is it possible to love enemies? And what would this look like?

5   What does it mean to help Jesus carry the cross?

6

The sins of the world

He carried the sins of the world.

He carried the harsh words that I reserve for those I love most. He carried the bruising resentfulness of my pride. He carried every one of the petty excuses that I use to defend myself. He carried the puffed-up charade of my vanity: my self-importance and my self-reliance. He carried every wrong decision I have ever made. He carried those moments of wilful wrong-doing, where I have stared down the right path, seen what it would cost me, and chosen the easy road instead.

He carried the time I took delight in seeing someone suffer. He carried the times I have bullied and cheated. He carried the time I stole, and the time I fiddled my expenses claim, and the many times I separated sex from love, and all the lies I told, and the hundreds of times I never said thank you, and the thousands of times I was so self-obsessed that I was blinded to the good that I could do.

Why, I even stood in the street as he walked by, carrying all this for me, and I did not notice him. I passed by. And he carried this as well. He carried my negligence and my envy. He carried my broken promises. He carried my deceit. He carried all those little hurts where I have let people down, where I have sat on the fence. He carried my cynicism: all my carefully rehearsed answers, put-downs, excuses; all my reasons for not caring, not believing, not trusting. He gathered up all the fragments of my conceit, every piece of bread that I refused to share – and the baskets he carried were overflowing.

O come to me all who are weary and overburdened . . .

And he carried the big, global horrors born of our pretentious complacency. He carried the melting ice caps and the ravaged rain forests of our plundering the earth, imagining it was ours to do with as we pleased. He carried the xenophobic fantasies that have bred the genocides and holocausts that litter our history. He carried the poisonous hatred that built Auschwitz and the arrogance that invaded Iraq. And the economies that thrive on division; and the poor whose plight is a necessary part of the equation that makes others rich; and the exploitation and degradation, and the corruption of power, he carried it all. The raped child and the bloody horror of the rapist – he carried it. Every hair on our sinful heads he counted and carried. All the idols we worship. All the things we do with our power and our wealth: the towers of Babel we build; the bombs we stockpile; the sophisticated ways that we kill each other, and the money we pour into finding new ways; the crucifixes we erect; the palaces we adorn for ourselves, and the thrones we set in place, and the walls we build around ourselves, and the sentries we post. Everything we construct to keep ourselves in and everyone else out: he carried it all. The divisions were so vast that they had to be dragged together, united in him, nailed down. He saw everything that separates me from us, and us from each other, and all of us from God, and he pulled it together and carried it. He picked it all up and he took it to the cross.

Ringing in his ears, he carried the frightened denials of Peter. Still wet upon his lips, he carried the moisture from Judas' kiss.

And as he went by we heaped more things upon him. We spat on him; we ridiculed him; we made fun of him; we gambled for his clothes; we jostled for a good view of his dying, or we fled in fear; and when he was thirsty we gave him vinegar to drink. And then we laughed at him some more.

This is what sin does. It isolates. It divides. It rules. It flourishes in the fertile ground of self-delusion, where every decision begins with me. It is an empire of isolation. It is to dwell in a crowded room and be completely alone.

And why does he carry this great weight? This impossible burden of everything that is warped and twisted? What possible good can come from it? Isn't this stupidity just one more reason to sneer?

The answer will shame us. Unless, that is, you have let cynicism get such a grip on your heart that there is no room left for love. For that is the answer: love.

For God so loved the world . . .

I came not to call the righteous . . .

The weight is unimaginable, but the arms that bear the weight are stronger still, and they are true. He carries them because he wants to get rid of them. He will take them to the cross and crucify them.

Father forgive them, they don't know what they do . . .

He will take them to the tomb and bury them. He will go on loving when all we can do is load insult upon injury. For this is what we do: we pass the buck, we blame each other, we evade the spotlight of responsibility, and we hide. We duck and weave. We squirm and sneer. And he carries it. He carries it for love. For when we say he carried the sins of the world, we mean *every* sin; and we mean that there is no such thing as a large sin or a small sin; and we mean every sin that

The sins of the world

separates us from each other, and we mean every sin that separates us from God; and we mean that sin is real; and most of all we mean *my* sins and *your* sins. It is all so horribly simple: I don't do the things I want to do. And I end up doing the things I don't want to do. I am compromised and defeated by all my wrong choices. I choose to call it something else, but I know it is sin. It is what I know to be wrong and I don't need God to know it. I am stranded. I am weighed down.

But if I look very closely I can see something else that he carries. Not just my sins as if they were separate from me (I am dead in my sin, I am not the person I want to be, I am already isolated and alone). He is carrying something else: carrying something which is very precious; something which needs to be restored; something which he knows can be beautiful; something which can be loved back to life. He carries me. And I am not heavy to him.

For reflection

Hold something that is broken. Something that seems impossible to mend, like the torn off petals of a flower: see if you can rearrange them. Feel how hopeless it is. Watch them fade.

If you are in a group, use just one flower. Take off the petals. Carefully pass them round. Try to reconstruct the flower or at least put it together in some way.

If you are on your own, break up the flower and having held it for a while try to reassemble it as best you can.

Read Romans 5.1–11. Then ask these questions:

1   How does it feel to be hopeless?

2   How might it feel to have things put back together, or re-created into something even more beautiful?

3   How does it feel to be forgiven?

4   How does it feel to be put back together?

5   What is sin? How does it spoil things?

6   What does it mean to say Jesus died for our sins?

7

Our sorrows

He carried our sorrows.

Nothing was too small for him. All the fragments were gathered up.

And nothing was too large or too heavy. He carried the tiny, casual disappointments, the lost hopes and shattered dreams that reverberate through a lifetime. And he carried the huge, ravaging hurts, where tragedy bites and the tectonic plates of a lifetime shift.

He carried the lives that are lost before they have hardly begun, the lives cut short, and the lives that are savagely realigned by grief or injury or abuse.

How can we list all this pain? How can we account for it? Only that we see it in his arms gathered together, carried: the pain of miscarriage, the lost potential of abortion; the confusion and indifference that cohere; the sudden inexplicable tragedies of so-called accidents; the friendly fire, the severed limbs, the collateral damage and all the unspectacular horrors of war; the steady deterioration of the body; the unhurried affliction of dementia; the howls of grief cried out at the never-ending hours of death; the emptiness of the days that follow; the creak of the gate; the footsteps on the path; the heartbeat knocking on the door; the unopened telegram; the phone unanswered in the hall; the torn fragments scattered in the fire; the dying embers offering up their heat, separating and departing; the crumbled earth dropping from our fingers as we step back from the graveside; the backward gaze that overshadows the evening of every life; and the stabbing intrusion of regret. He cradled them. Each was handled with a patient gentleness and an understanding that only comes from one who has known sorrow himself.

And gazing from the cross itself he saw it. All the failure and all the pain bound up together, and how one often feeds upon the other, so that the abuse of one life begets the abuse of another, victim and abuser bound together in a terrible cycle of horror and pain. And he did not make excuses, nor pretend that all the knotted skeins of our lives could be unravelled, smoothed out, understood. He saw us for what we are. And he loved us. And his words – and now unreservedly in his eyes – offered compassion, forgiveness. Not that you need to be forgiven for pain. But for all of us it is muddled together. He had the keys of the kingdom in one pierced hand and the balm of healing in the other. And he brought us both of them. He carried them.

He was a man of sorrows and acquainted with grief . . .

He was oppressed and he was afflicted . . .

He carried our fears; and he knew about fear. The sweat had poured from his body, and with it great drops of blood. He had been without food and drink. He had faced it down.

He carried our sorrow, and he knew about sorrow. He wept at the grave of his dear friend Lazarus. When he beheld the city, Jerusalem, that had killed so many prophets and turned its back on God, he wept. He embraced the lost and lonely. He held the frightened in his arms. He slipped his hand into the hands of tiny children and he comforted them. He broke his bread with those who are excluded and rejected by the world. He crossed boundaries. He sat down in exclusion zones. He sought out the very ones the rest of us had hidden away. He felt the pain of difference and indifference, of nepotism and of prohibition. He overturned tables and he broke down barriers. He upended expectations. He was never what anyone wanted him to be. And so he carried his own sorrow, knowing that to please God meant the displeasure of everyone else, and then their contempt heaped upon him. For that was what they did now – all their rile, their rancour, their ridicule and their rage they poured upon him; they sought to devour him, to bury him, to destroy him. But even this – this naked perversity – he carried it. He saw the uncovered countenance of evil and he wept with sorrow, cried out in forgiveness, embraced it, carried it, drew its sting into himself, and defeated it.

He carried our doubts and he knew about doubt. Knew it was a part of faith: the necessary reverse of the coin. He had wrestled in the garden. He had faced the seductions of evil – the beguiling comforts of an easier road. And hardly able to believe that he is carrying us, and torn apart by our limitations, he carries doubt, his and mine and yours, carries the very doubt that looks at him, wonders whether he has anything save a certain charismatic madness, and turns away.

For reflection

Hold an empty basket. Imagine it being filled with the fears, sorrows, doubts and anxieties of your life and of every life. Imagine all this being held, carried and understood. Imagine the love that would do such a thing.

If you are in a group, you may either do this by passing the basket around, or by placing the basket in the middle and inviting people to write down what they would like held, which they then place in the basket.

If you are on your own, either just hold the basket and think about it, or write things down which you can place in it.

Then try to remember back to being held yourself. Recall a childhood memory of being lifted up, or twirled around, or being carried to bed.

If you are in a group, share these memories.

If you are on your own, just think about them.

Read Romans 8.18–39. Then ask these questions:

1   How does it feel to be carried? What does it mean?

2   How does it feel to be lost, or to suffer the pain of being dropped?

3   What does pain do to us?

4   What does it mean to say Jesus shared the pain and
     sorrow of the world?

8

A broken heart

He carried a heart that was about to be broken.

That was how he eventually died. He carried his heart, open and vulnerable, from Jordan to Jerusalem, from Gethsemane to Golgotha. And then it was broken: broken by the savagery of the death he was about to face; broken by the sheer, uncompromising weight of all the other things he carried; but most of all, broken by the love that brought him to this moment of self-surrender.

Things slot into place. The halves of the cross are put together. Nailed down, weighed down, strung up – but also lifted up – boiled in the heat of the sun, shifting his weight from nailed wrists to nailed feet, facing the tortuous choice between suffocation and rending pain, the last hours of his life begin.

He looks again at his mother. She is just standing there, a sword of pain piercing her heart too. He sees the beloved apostle John and a few other women from his group. Everyone else has gone. There is a terrible loneliness in dying.

The hours pass. A strange overshadowing darkness creeps over the land. Suddenly there is a chill in the air. The noisy heckling of the crowd gives way to boredom and silence. One of the soldiers nods off. Some of the crowd start to drift away. The show is nearly over. Those who thought something spectacular might happen depart, disappointed, but not really surprised. There is business to be getting on with. The torturer's horse scratches its innocent behind on a tree.

The agony is now at its worst. His temperature soars. His eyes swim. Disjointed, he heaves upward to gasp another breath. Everything is fading. Sweat peppers his body. Blood flows. He gasps with thirst. Rasping and raging.

I am thirsty ...

Carrying so much, and the pain so great; and still the fear, also raging, still fermenting, nearly all-consuming, that he is actually carrying nothing, that it is all to no avail.

Who is it watching?

Who placed this thing here?

Who is waiting?

Why this cup in this moment?

Everything disjointed.
Stretching.
His body starting to fail.
Falter.
His ability to resist starting to fade.
Expiring.
No longer carrying the will to live.
Abandoned now.
The weariness from the beating.
It takes its toll.
It consumes you.
Now diminishing.
The barometer crashing.
The distant thunder rising.
Blood pressure falling.
Heart pounding.
Faster.
Faster.
The end in sight.
His lungs fill with fluid.
Gurgling, poisoning.
It is like he has taken a big breath in, but can never
    breathe out again.
He holds it there, is held there, blown up, kippered,
    racked.
His body clinging to life, but the grip slipping.
He will slide away now.
He will be done with.

This is the awful truth that dawns on the few who see him there: he cannot carry his life any longer. Death rattles in the parched emptiness of his throat and, eventually, crying out in thirst, the condemned man dies. His heart breaks.

Then there is silence. Deaths like these always cheat the onlookers of a defining moment. They are still watching, they are still waiting. Their vigil continues, as if the death has not yet arrived, as if it could still be cheated.

The soldiers fidget impatiently, wanting to get home.

The religious leaders and the politicians wait anxiously, wanting to hear that it is over, coveting normality, smoothing things over. Their calendar hasn't changed.

Jerusalem is in a kind of repressed ferment. There is anger and excitement and indignation. People tell their versions of events. Some feel guilty about what they have or haven't done. They talk about what has happened. Few think anything much will happen next. The Sabbath is approaching, and for those who only long for the status quo to be resumed Jesus is still a problem.

Everyone agrees this: it would be much better to bring things to a close, to have done with it. Place a full stop on the sentence of this deluded life. So the religious leaders barter with Pilate, and the soldiers are told to bring the cycle of suffering to an end: break the legs of the crucified men. This is not the act of additional cruelty it may appear, but an errand of mercy. Breaking the legs enables death to come swiftly: no more time can be purchased. The shifting of weight from wrists to feet will be ended. The pressure on the chest un-relieved. But when they get to Jesus, when they make to break his legs, they find he is already dead.

Unless a grain of wheat falls in the ground . . .

Now we see another mystery – long carried, hidden but secure – come into the light. It is germinating. The soldiers need to be sure. One of them lifts a spear. And to make sure he's dead pierces his side.

This is the real moment of disclosure; the moment when the balance tips, or when the slowly turning focus of the lens brings everything into sharp clarity. We see with astonished elation that something else is happening. As if in slow motion. The spear pressed violently into his heart. With-drawn. It is obvious he is dead. But it is also obvious that it is not over. The tiniest flickering of a movement: not life, but something else. Something which isn't death and isn't life, not this 'in, out, pulsating, fleshly, slowly expiring life', but a different sort of living, something that is coming from this broken heart and connecting with every heart that ever beat or broke. First, a tiny spot of blood; then a droplet of water. It washes from his heart: two tiny streams. It is an awakening, a flowering. It is hardly discernible, not recognizable: you could pass it by a thousand times, and yet at the same time, in my mind's eye, through this lens, a mighty river, coming out of heaven to earth, a new creation: water and blood streaming from his heart to mine.

Now I see what he carried. I see the weight of it. I see what was always at the heart of it. An irrigation and an invitation and a choice. This is where I can be refreshed. This is where I can be fed. This is the place where burdens are relieved. This is a path to follow.

And I am either defiled by this weight, refusing the invitation, remaining stubbornly locked in my barren dryness, or I am purified by it, entering into it, accepting it. And if I had hours to reflect on it I would say, I go down into the waters. I am drenched in them, drowned in them, washed in them, warmed in them. I travel through the dark portals of death and I rise with him. I drink this blood, and like a child at its mother's breast receive the nourishment I need, life feeding on life. I am refreshed. I am reconfigured. I am reborn. But I don't have time for reflection: it is as if for a moment he has stepped back from dying and shown me a new living, and what I actually feel is this: I look at the dead Jesus hanging on the cross, and the water and blood flowing from his side, and it feels like he picks me up. He is carrying me. But not just because I have fallen and the way is hard; he is carrying me *somewhere*: to these living waters, to this shed blood, to this place of refreshment, to a new creation; and a new reality. These are the waters where I can be washed clean. This is the table where I am the honoured guest. This is where I get up.

His heart is broken for me. His love holds me to himself and holds himself to that cross with a greater strength than any nail could ever muster. We are crucified with him and we are carried by him.

So here I stand. It is as if everyone else has departed and I am alone at the foot of the cross. The day is almost over, and Jesus waits upon me. He looks at me with such tenderness. He won't make this decision for me. He just waits. And until that day when God gathers together all the scattered fragments of his creation he will go on waiting. His offer remains the same, There is nothing I need to do to earn it or deserve it. It is just there, carried by this cross. I feel the weight of it. I see the extent of it; and I am faced with a choice. It is the same choice that every person faces or avoids; the same choice those criminals either side of him encountered as their lives inched towards death: shall we sneer, or shall we ask to be remembered?

For reflection

Hold a small wooden cross. First, let it rest in the palm of your hand, then fold your fingers around it. Just hold it and think about what it means and what it carries.

If you are in a group, you could either pass one cross around, or if you are able to get hold of enough small crosses have each person hold one at the same time. For the cross is one and it is for everyone.

If you are on your own, just hold the cross and think about it.

Read John 19.28–37. Then ask these questions:

1   How does it feel to be loved? Share stories of falling in love or receiving love.

2   How does it feel to be found? Share stories of being lost and of being recovered.

3   What does it mean to say we are saved by the cross of Christ?

Finally, take hold of a jug of water and a bottle of wine. Hold them for a minute. Pour the water into a large bowl and then splash the water on your face. Open the wine and pour it into a large glass. Drink the wine.

If you are in a group, do this together in silence. When the water has been poured into the bowl wash your face in turn. Once the wine is poured out pass the glass from one person to the next.

If you are on your own, just quietly act out this ritual.

Think about the blood and water that flowed from Christ's heart: what they represent and the promises they offer.

If you are in a group and there are enough crosses for each person invite people to take one home.

A prayer

Loving God,
your Son Jesus Christ carried us to the cross
and shed his blood for us and brought us into
    new community with you:

help us to follow in his way,
deny ourselves and take up the cross he gives us,
that the world may learn his way of peace;

may his life and his purposes be alive in us this day,
and may we be alive in him;

and when our hearts are broken,
and when the burdens of this life feel too great to bear,
take us to the cross,
and enable us to see there the great weight that
    Jesus carried;
for here we receive the affirmation of your love,
the assurance of your promise,
and the strength to persevere.

For we ask it in his name.
Amen.

Excerpt from the follow-up volume, *The Things He Said*

The two of them stand in the garden. The sun is just beginning to cast the fullness of its first rays across the dew-drenched earth.

She is standing in front of the tomb. Her body is still, but deep unrest convulses her spirit. Tears smudge her face. The stone that was placed at the entrance is pushed away to one side. He is standing beside her. Close to her, but not quite next to her. She is sort of half-turned round, looking at him, wondering who he is and where he came from. They can see each other clearly and they look at each other closely, but she is not turning round to face him properly. She has no idea who he is. And yet she has this strange desire to reach out to him. It seems as if he might know something.

She sees but doesn't see. She hears but doesn't hear. Like many before her, like so many after, she doesn't get it. Not yet. He is standing before her – the very one whom she is looking for – but she doesn't know it is him. Perhaps the early morning sun is in her eyes? Perhaps her tears have blurred her vision? Or is it something else?

'Who are you looking for?' he says.

Such a question. And she didn't know there was any more feeling to be dredged from the pit of her heart. But this question burns like fire. There is so much she is looking for, but in these last few weeks it had all focused itself into one person – into him – the one whose lifeless corpse she was seeking, the one she didn't know she was looking for until she found him, although even then it seemed as though he had always been looking for her. That was how it was for everyone who found him – who was found by him – his words and his presence seemed to chime with the deepest longings of the heart, not taking away all the other questions, but re-framing them within the knowledge of a great love, and the astonishing relief of receiving affirmation. To be loved and accepted; that was what no one else had ever given her in life – not without condition – and she didn't even know how much she wanted it (how badly she needed it) until it was found. Found in him.

'Who are you looking for?' She wanted to cry out: 'I am looking for the one who saved me. Isn't it obvious? The one who taught me how to be myself. Who accepted me. Who gave meaning back to me. Who put a spring in my stride. Who showed me other ways of living, and who taught me joy beyond possession, and who rid my world of fear.'

She had followed him. From the first moment she had heard of him to the day when she encountered him, to his un-equivocal acceptance of her, and his protection when others had scoffed and scorned. She had sought him out. She stood behind him in the house of that self-satisfied Pharisee and she had wept.

How strange! She had wept then as she was weeping now. And as her tears had fallen she had knelt at his feet and bathed them with her tears and dried them with her hair. Then she had kissed his feet and, breaking open the jar of ointment she had brought with her, she had anointed his feet. She shuddered with the memory. Those feet she had held, skewered to a cross.

Now when the Pharisee who had invited him saw this, he was full of righteous indignation. What is it about the religious, she thought, that they are so quick to judge? They take such delight in it. He puffed himself up. He was a proper, 'pleased with himself' man of God, knowing all there was to be known about the failings of others. He knew the location of every splinter. 'If this man were a prophet,' he said, looking around himself proudly, anticipating the applause, milking it, 'he would know what kind of woman this is who is touching him.' And she remembered his pointing finger, his condescending tone, his lascivious eye. If he could not touch her himself, he would make damn sure that anyone else who did was contaminated in his place. And it wasn't as if she had never experienced this before. No one was ever neutral about those in her trade. But it was worse in the presence of this accepting man, whose feet she held, because he had been pleased to receive her service – that was all – and this condemnation sullied him.

But he was never a weak man. And always impeccably mannered, always sure. He spoke back. 'May I say something to you?' he asked.

Another of his strange stories – a riddle: a certain creditor with two debtors, one owing 500 denarii, the other 50. Neither can pay. Both debts are cancelled.

'Which one will love him more?' he asks, nonchalantly, almost innocently. And the faintest whisper of a smile chances across his face. He leads them to condemn themselves. That was part of the mystery of his goodness. He never condemned anyone himself, just kept on pointing out the truth of things, till you either saw it yourself – God so loved the world – or crushed him in your rage. Which is, in the end, what they did. The logic of unfailing charity was always going to be too much to bear for those who had spent a lifetime avoiding it.

'I suppose the one for whom he cancelled the greater debt,' came back the reply.

And then he did smile. Not rudely. Not grinning. But an actual smile that even here recognition might dawn, hearts could be changed. That was what he was always after. He wanted to save them all. 'You have judged rightly,' he said.

And then he had turned to her: 'Do you see this woman? I entered your house; you gave me no water for my feet, but she has bathed my feet with her hair. You gave me no kiss, but from the time I came in she has not stopped kissing my feet.